AF428390

Fun Facts about Nitrogen

Chemistry for Kids

The Element Series

Children's Chemistry Books

BABY PROFESSOR

EDUCATION KIDS

Speedy Publishing LLC
40 E. Main St. #1156
Newark, DE 19711
www.speedypublishing.com

Nitrogen is an important element for the survival of animals and plants. This process is known as the Nitrogen Cycle. It also plays a part in the air we breathe. We will be discussing additional characteristics and properties as well as providing additional information about this chemical element.

Characteristics and Properties of Nitrogen

It is found on the periodic table in column 15. It is the first element listed in that column. It is grouped as a nonmetal element as "other". Its atoms consist of 7 protons and 7 electrons and 5 of its electrons are on its outer shell.

7

N

Nitrogen

14.007

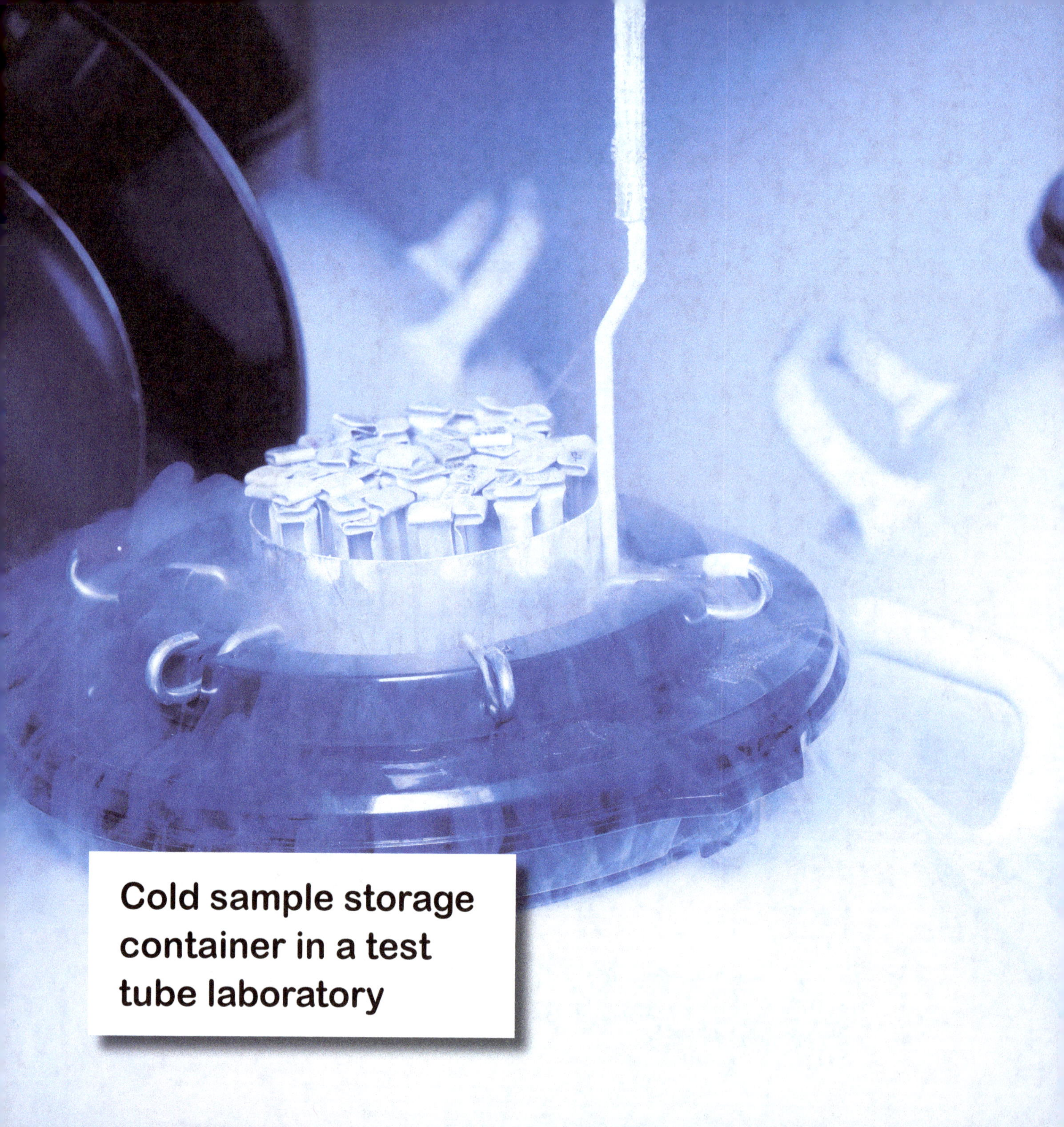

Cold sample storage container in a test tube laboratory

It its standard state it is a tasteless, odorless, and colorless gas. It forms into diatomic molecules which means there are 2 nitrogen atoms per molecule contained in nitrogen gas (N2). In this state, it is quite inert, which means it does not react with other compounds. It becomes liquid at -210 degrees Celsius. In its liquid form, it appears as water. Some familiar compounds containing nitrogen include nitrates, nitrites, nitrous oxide, and ammonia. Organic compounds including amines, amides, and nitro groups also contain Nitrogen.

Nitrogen - 14 and nitrogen-15 are its 2 stable isotopes. More than 99% of the nitrogen in our universe is nitrogen-14. There is a sickness known as decompression sickness which occurs when its bubbles form in our bloodstream. This is sometimes referred to as the bends and takes place when a scuba diver rises to the surface of the water too quickly when diving. It can also occur with astronauts and people working in an unpressurized aircraft.

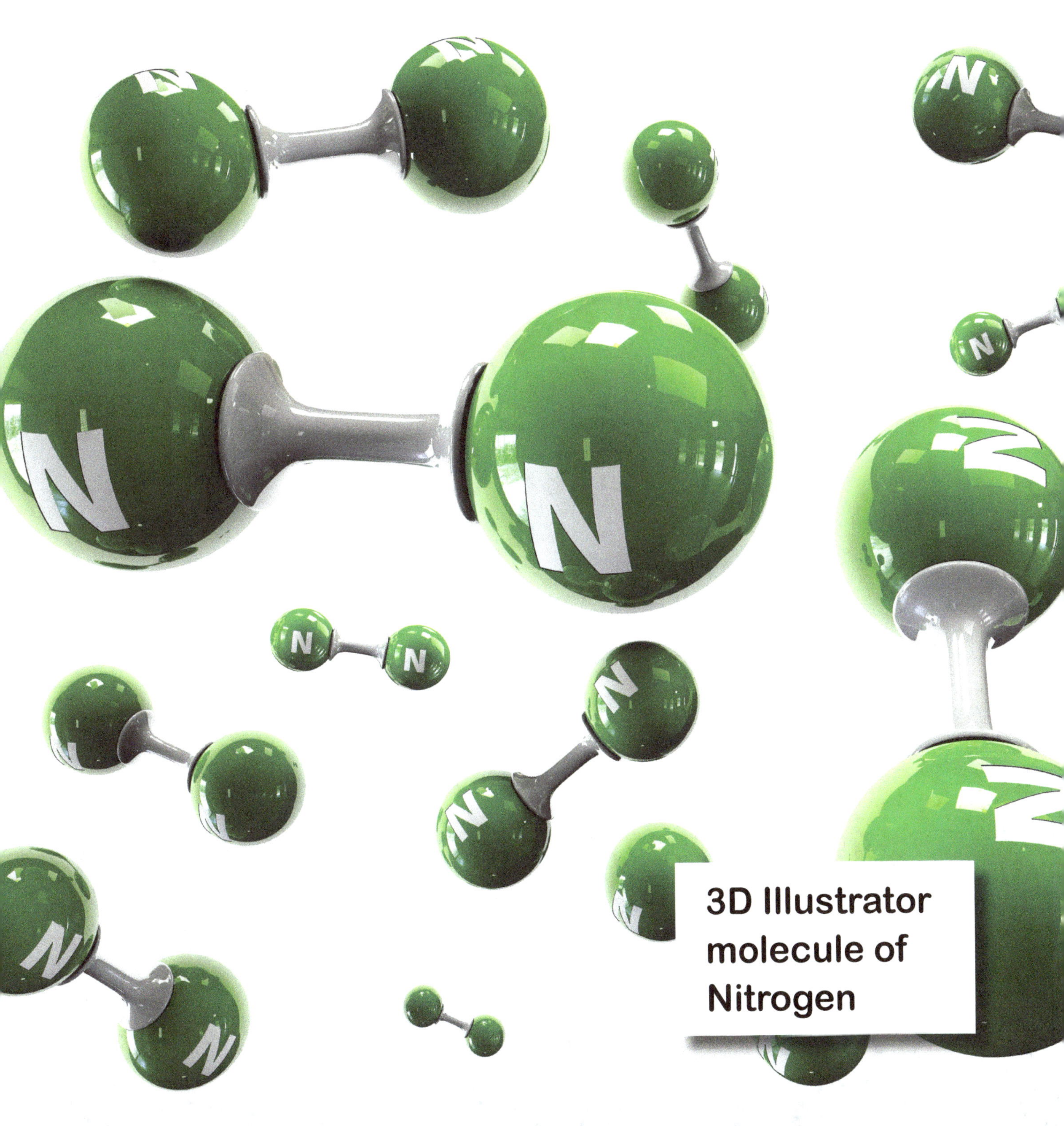

3D Illustrator
molecule of
Nitrogen

Fertilizers on
young plant

Where is it Found?

Even though we refer to air as oxygen, it is made up mostly of nitrogen. Our atmosphere is comprised of 78% its gas, otherwise known as N2. While the air is comprised most of it, very little is found on the crust of the Earth. A few rare minerals including saltpeter do contain it. All living things, including animals and plants, need it. It also is needed in nucleic acids and proteins. Think about it the next time you are breathing outside, or admiring the beauty of plants.

What are its Uses?

Its primary use is to make ammonia for industry. When we combine hydrogen with it to make ammonia, this process is named the Haber process. The resulting ammonia can then be used to make explosives, fertilizers, and nitric acid. TNT, nitroglycerin, and gunpowder are some of the explosives that contain nitrogen. It is also used to preserve foods, in manufacturing, reduces fire hazards, and is used in light bulbs that are incandescent.

Machine spreading
liquid manure

Refrigerators use it in its liquid form to keep food cold. Blood and biological samples are preserved with nitrogen. It is also used by scientists to perform experiments under low temperatures. Its gas is useful for keeping beer pressured in kegs. It produces smaller bubbles which is preferred in some brands of beer.

Amber colored
carbonated
bubbles

Planet Saturn

Saturn's largest moon, known as Titan, has an atmosphere consisting of more than 98% nitrogen. This makes it the only moon known to have this dense of an atmosphere.

The lives of animals and plants depend on it. It is also a major part of several processes and cells including proteins, amino acids, and our DNA. Photosynthesis of plants depends on it for their food.

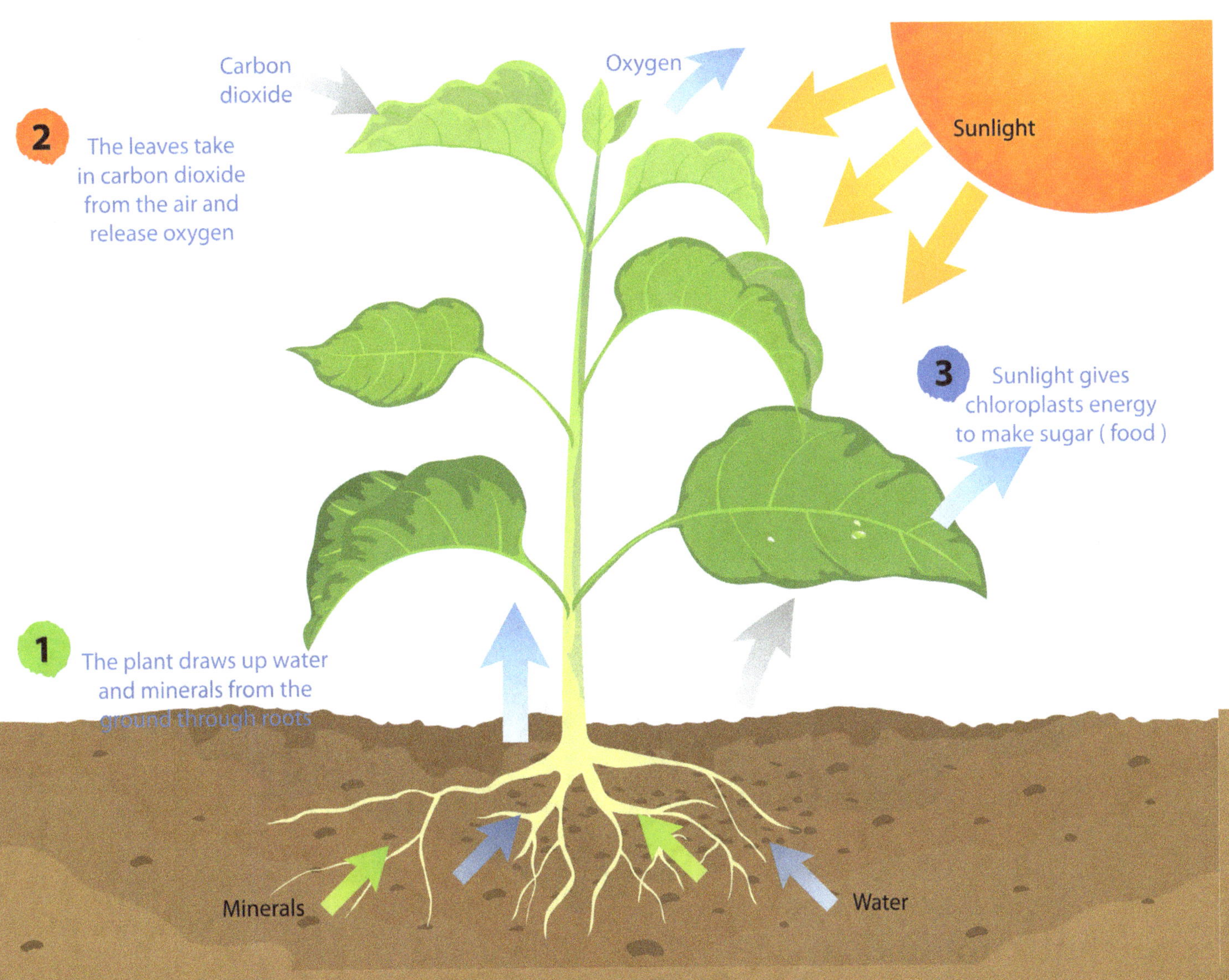

Carbon dioxide
Oxygen
Sunlight
2
The leaves take in carbon dioxide from the air and release oxygen
3
Sunlight gives chloroplasts energy to make sugar (food)
1
The plant draws up water and minerals from the ground through roots
Minerals
Water

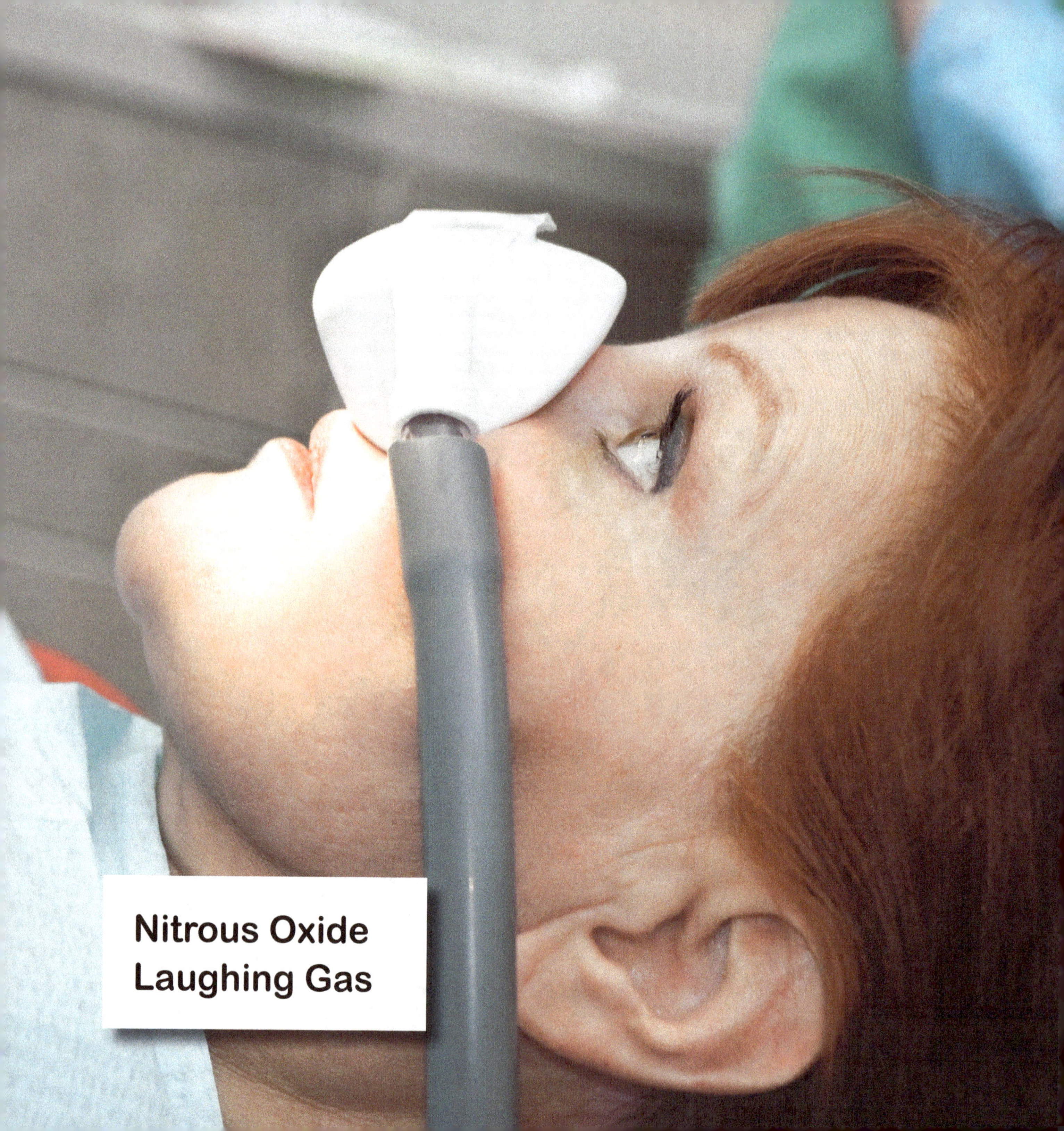
Nitrous Oxide
Laughing Gas

In hospitals and dentists' office, nitrous oxide (N2O), often referred to as laughing gas, is used for anesthesia so as to reduce pain and awareness for various procedures. It is also used to increase power and speed in motor racing. It is known as NOS when used for racing. It is considered as an air pollutant and greenhouse gas. Its weight is almost 300 times than that of carbon dioxide.

Its Beginning

In 1772, Daniel Rutherford, a Scottish chemist, first isolated nitrogen. He referred to it as noxious air.

NITROGEN
READ PRODUCT WARNING LABEL AND MATERIAL SAFETY DATA SHEET. DO NOT REMOVE OUTLET FITTINGS. DO NOT TAMPER WITH SETTINGS.
NITROGEN
REFRIGERATED LIQUID
UN 1977
ALWAYS KEEP CONTAINER IN UPRIGHT POSITION.
WARNING
FIRST AID
EXTREMELY COLD LIQUID AND GAS
UNDER PRESSURE.
CAN CAUSE RAPID SU

Molecular chef

In 1790, a French chemist named Jean-Antoine Chaptel named it after a mineral niter when he discovered that the gas contained niter. Niter is also referred to as potassium nitrate or saltpeter. Carl William Scheele and Henry Cavendish also discovered it around the same time. Since Rutherford published his work about it first, he receives the credit for its discovery.

The Nitrogen Cycle

The process that causes it to move in between animals, plants, atmosphere, bacteria, and soil is known as the nitrogen cycle. All life as we know it on Earth is dependent on it.

Nitrogen Fixation
$N_2 + 8H^+ + 8e^- \rightarrow 2NH_3 + H_2$
N_2

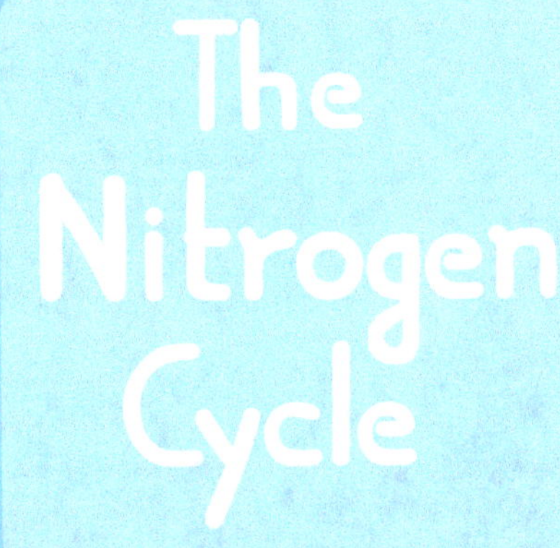

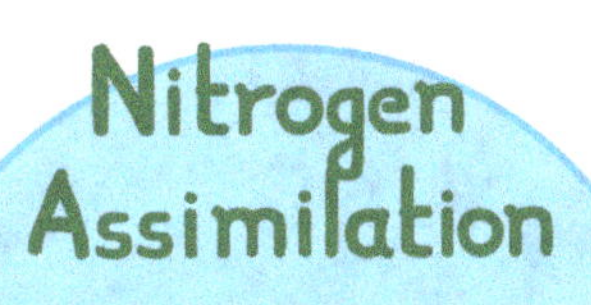

The Nitrogen Cycle

Nitrogen Assimilation
NO_2
NO_3

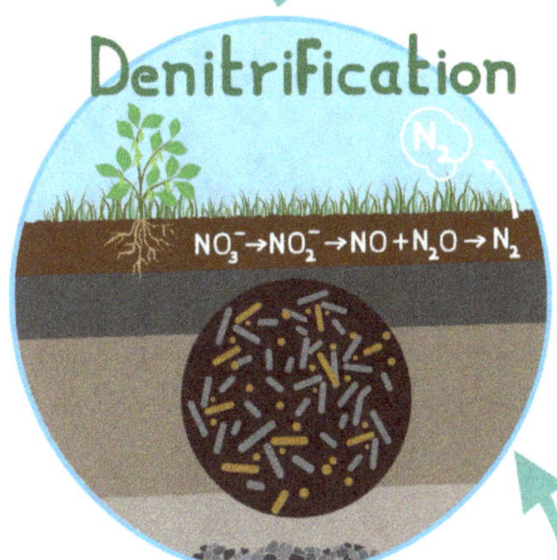

Denitrification
N_2
$NO_3^- \rightarrow NO_2^- \rightarrow NO + N_2O \rightarrow N_2$

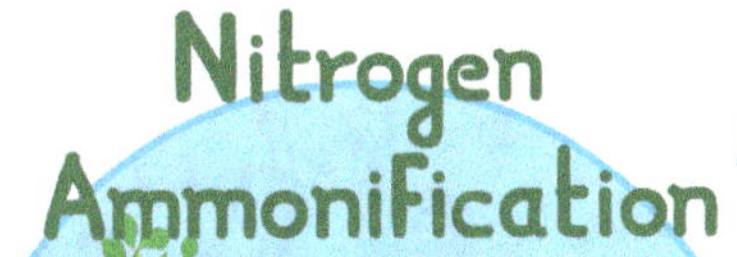

Nitrogen Ammonification
NH_4^+

Nitrification
$NH_3 + O_2 \rightarrow NO_2^- + 3H^+ + 2e^-$
$NO_2^- + H_2O \rightarrow NO_3^- + 2H^+ + 2e^-$

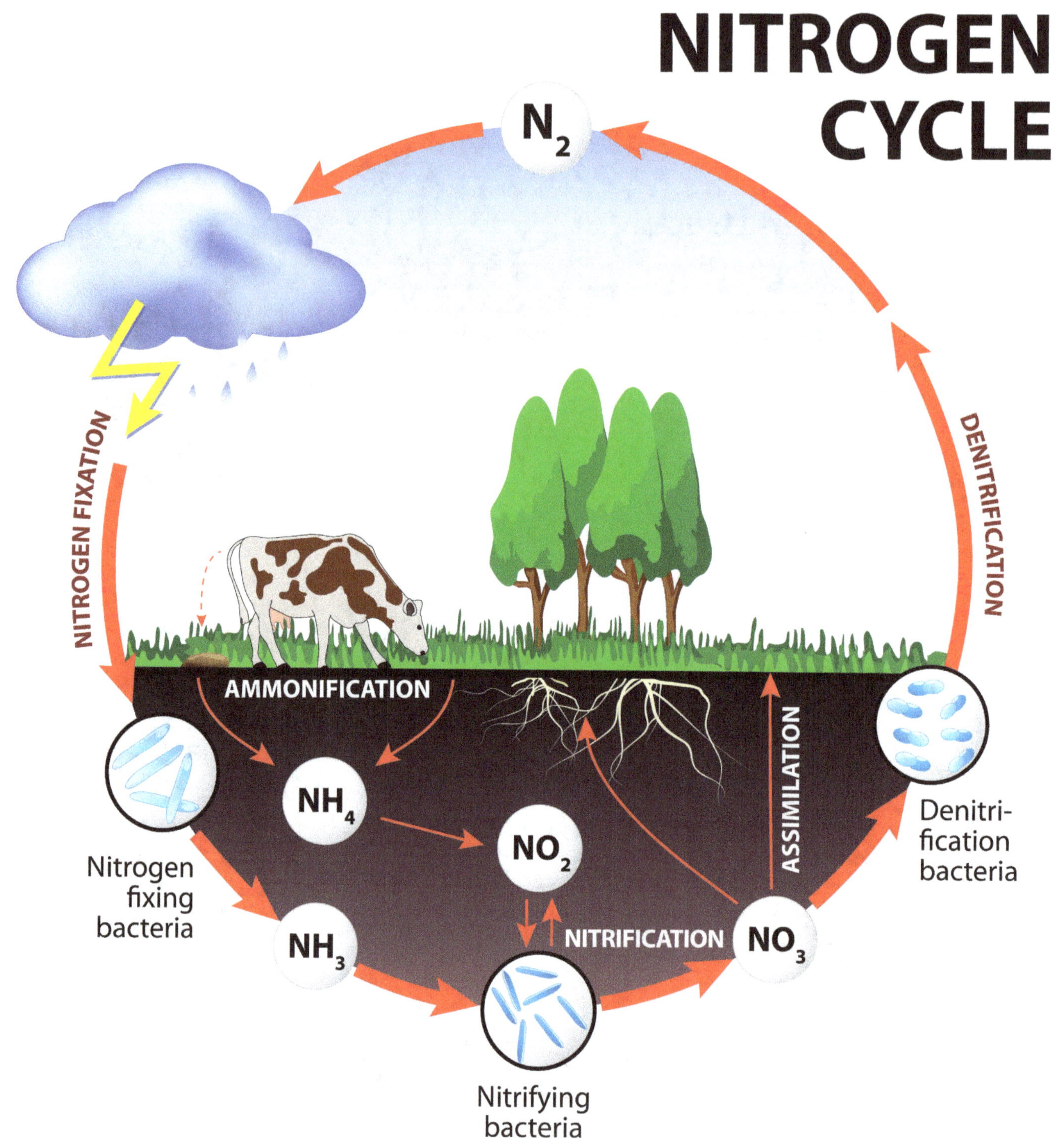

NITROGEN CYCLE
N2
NITROGEN FIXATION
DENITRIFICATION
AMMONIFICATION
ASSIMILATION
NH4
NH3
NO2
NO3
NITRIFICATION
Nitrogen fixing bacteria
Nitrifying bacteria
Denitrification bacteria

It must change to different states to be used in the various forms necessary for life on Earth. To be used it changes into various states in our atmosphere and is known as N2. it also forms into nitrates, nitrites and ammonium.

Bacteria is its most important part to the cycle. It helps it to change states so that it can be utilized. When it is absorbed into the soil, the bacteria help it to change states so that plants can absorb it. Plants then provide nitrogen for animals.

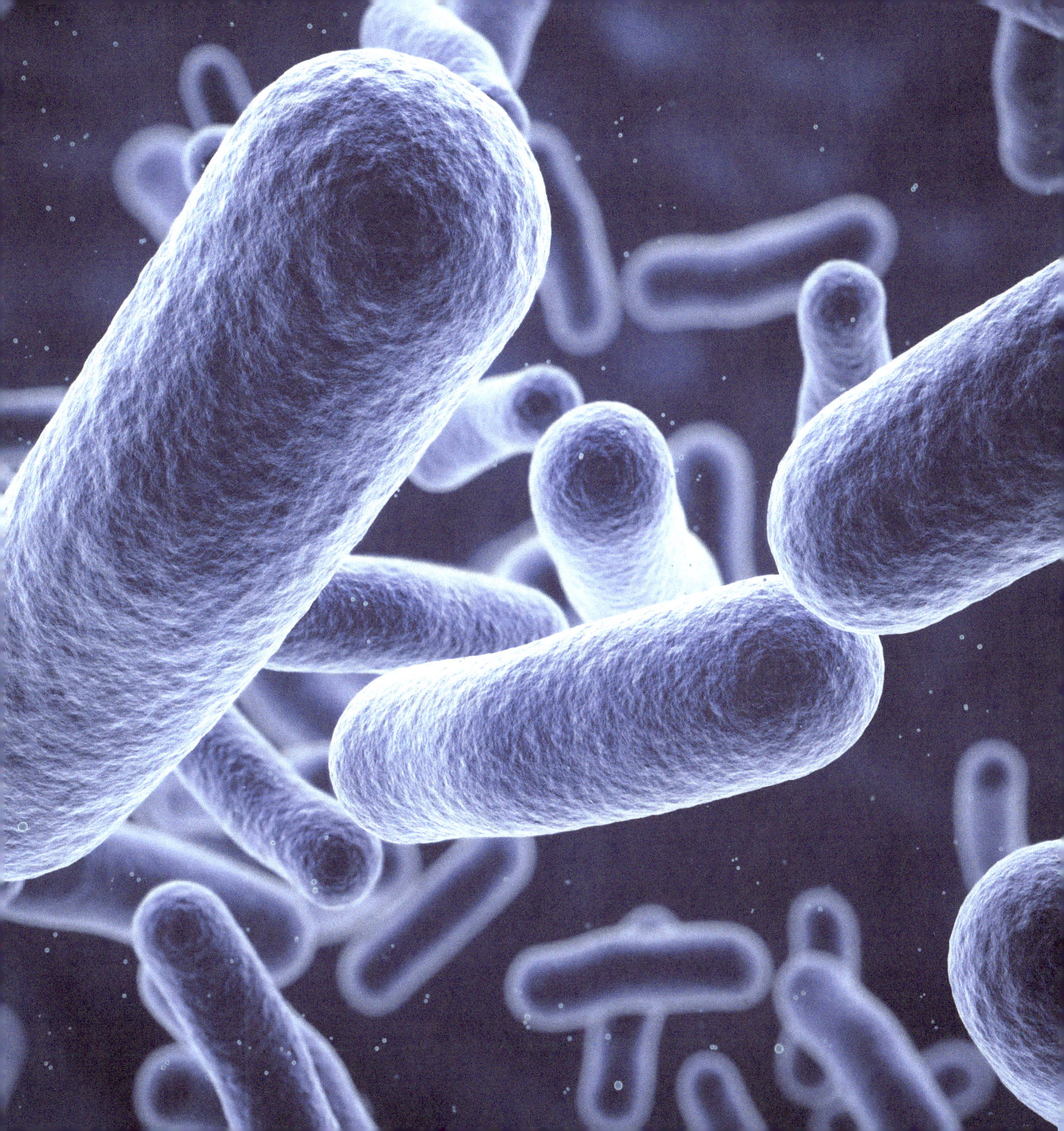

THE NITROGEN CYCLE

The process in the cycle are Fixation, Nitrification, Assimilation, Ammonification, and Denitrification. The definitions of each process are listed here:

The first step in this process is Fixation. This step makes sure that it is in a state that plants can use. Bacteria changes it to ammonium. The process where ammonium is changed to nitrates by bacteria is called Nitrification. Plants then absorb the nitrates.

Green plants
surrounding
the pond

Plants obtain it by Assimilation. The nitrates are absorbed into the soil and then to their roots. The nitrogen is used as amino acids, chlorophyll, and nucleic acids for the plants. The decaying process is known as Ammonification. As an animal or plant dies, fungi and bacteria act as decomposers turning the nitrogen to ammonium so it can return to the cycle.

As the remaining nitrogen is returned from the soil to the air assisted with certain bacteria, this process is known as Denitrification.

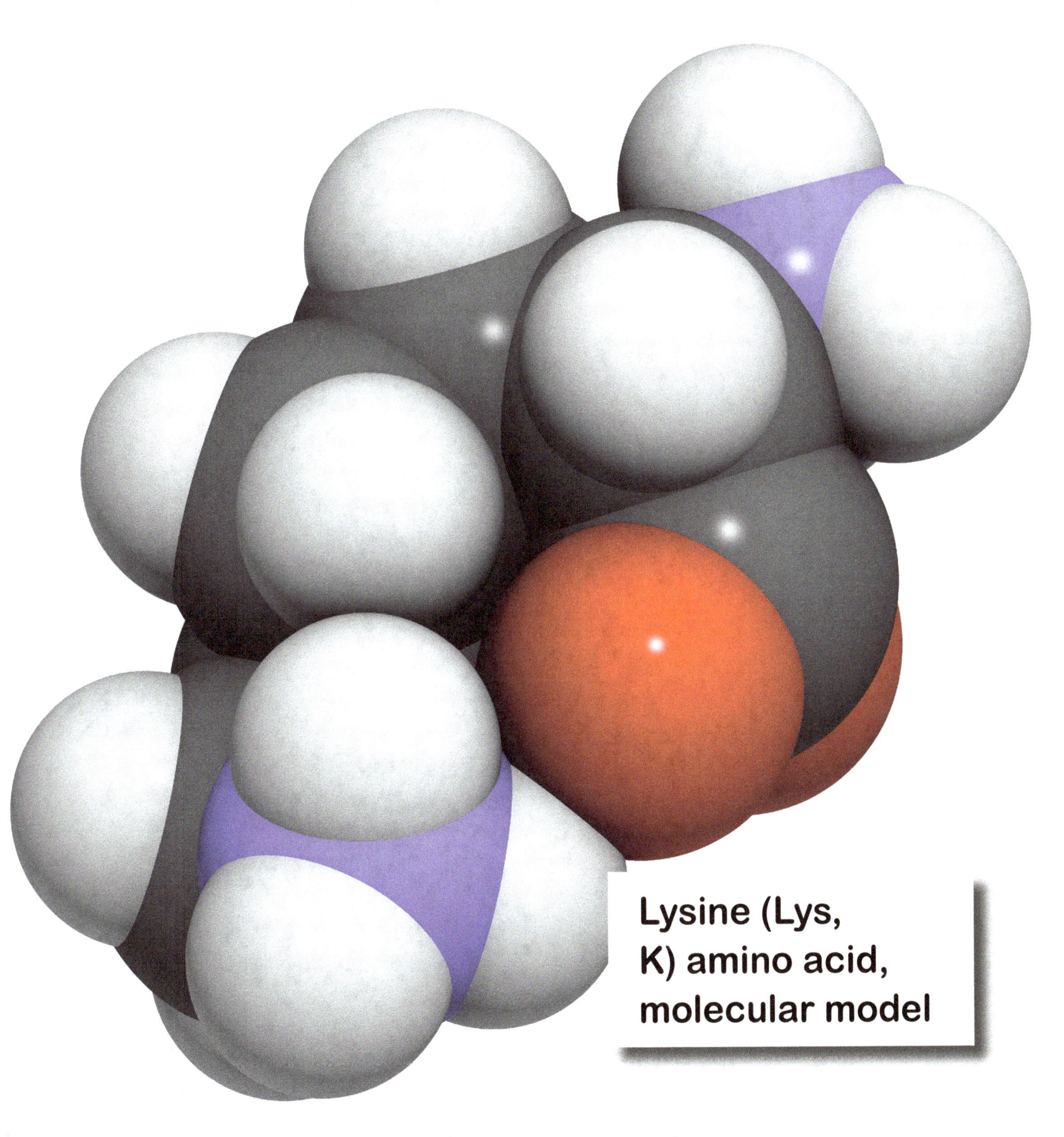

Lysine (Lys, K) amino acid, molecular model

Unfortunately, the cycle has been altered by the activity of human beings. this occurs when nitrogen is added to the soil is fertilized fertilizer and different activities that add its gas and to the atmosphere.

Liquid Nitrogen

In its liquid state, it becomes very cold. It is industrially produced by the fractionally distillation of the liquid air. It becomes a clear, colorless liquid with a density of 0.807 g/ml when it reaches it boiling point and has a dielectric constant at 1.43. It becomes so cold since it boils at -320 degrees Fahrenheit. Since it presents as a gas when at room temperature, it is necessary for it to be in its liquid state which is very cold. In its liquid state, it is so cold that it will freeze your skin as soon as it becomes in contact with it and cause severe damage.

Liquid nitrogen
pouring on surface

Sample storage
in test-tube
laboratory

It can be stored and transported when insulated well from ambient heat. Its temperature is held at 77 K by a slow boiling of the liquid, which results in a gas state.

While you may think that the cloud has something to do with the poisonous gas, it is simply the same as fog. It is cold and the air gets close and the water vapor contained in the air causes condensation which results in the tiny drops that remain suspended.

Research Series

Nitrogen

Is it combustible? It is considered an inert gas, which are not combustible and do not burn. Other chemicals in this group are neon, helium, krypton, and argon.

Before it can be used to eat or drink, it must be totally evaporated. While it is safe to use in preparation of food and drinks, it should not be ingested. If you search the internet you will find an experiment on how to make ice cream with it. Do not attempt this experiment without an adult present.

Liquid nitrogen ice cream

Nitrogen

By itself, liquid nitrogen is extremely cheap. However, a hospital tank can run up to $999. Can you imagine how much a larger tank would cost?

Periodic Table of Elements

There is so much more to learn about this element as well as the many other elements. You may want to research the periodic table of elements which lists all the elements including their atomic structure. In 1869, a Russian chemist named Dmitri Mendeleev came up with this table. With the use of this table, he had the ability to predict properties of elements prior to them being discovered.

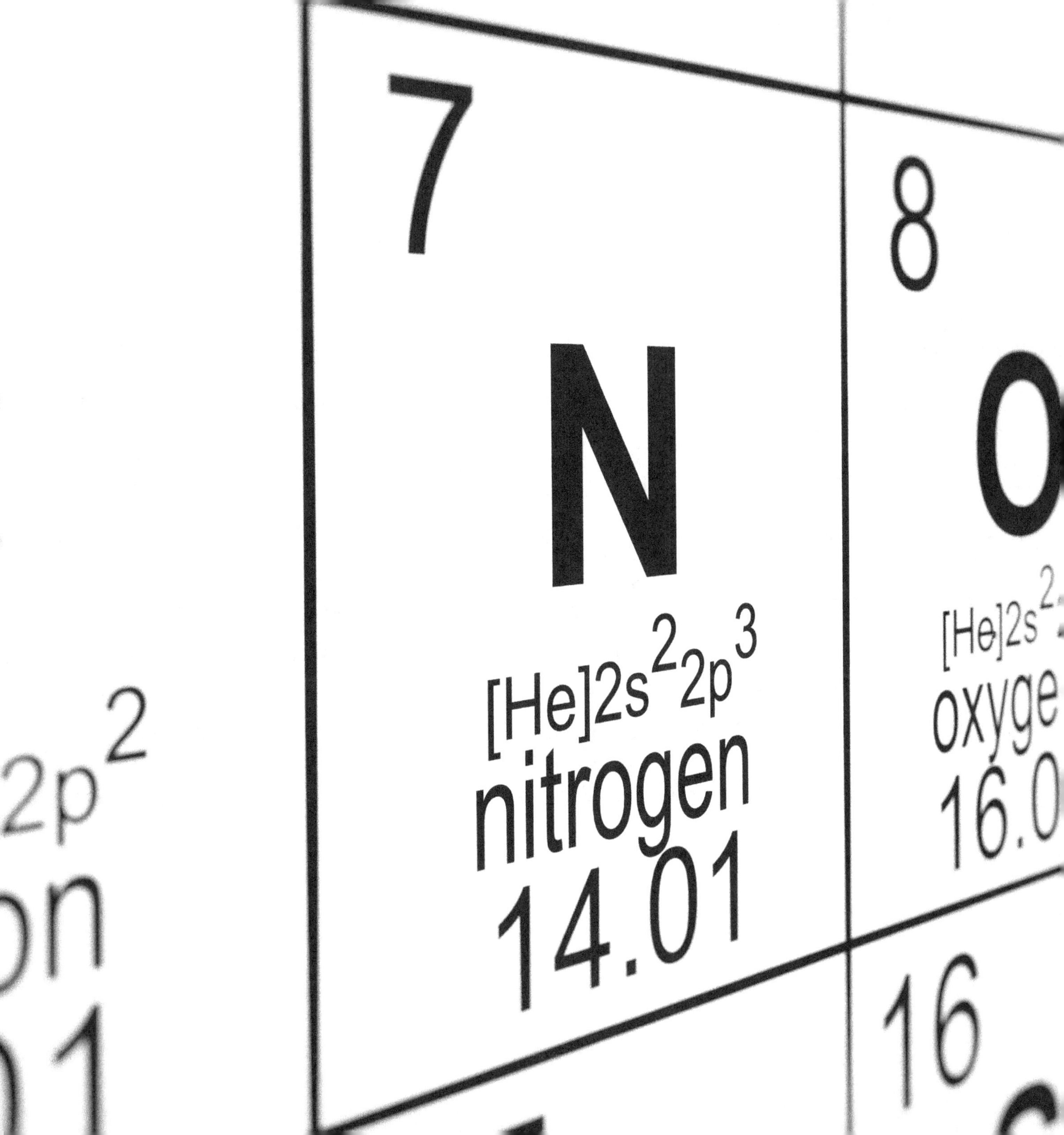

7
N
[He]2s² 2p³
nitrogen
14.01
8
O
[He]2s²
oxyge
16.0

PERIODIC TABLE OF THE ELEMENTS

Non-metal
Alkali metal
Alkaline earth metal
Transition metal

Metal
Metalloid
Halogen

Noble gas
Lanthanide
Actinide

1 H HYDROGEN 1.0079																	2 He HELIUM 4.0
3 Li LITHIUM 6.941	4 Be BERYLLIUM 9.0122											5 B BORON 10.811	6 C CARBON 12.011	7 N NITROGEN 14.007	8 O OXYGEN 15.999	9 F FLUORINE 18.998	10 Ne NEON 20.1
11 Na SODIUM 22.989	12 Mg MAGNESIUM 24.305											13 Al ALUMINIUM 26.981	14 Si SILICON 28.085	15 P PHOSPHORUS 30.974	16 S SULFUR 32.066	17 Cl CHLORINE 35.453	18 Ar ARGON 39.9
19 K POTASSIUM 39.098	20 Ca CALCIUM 40.078	21 Sc SCANDIUM 44.955	22 Ti TITANIUM 47.867	23 V VANADIUM 50.9415	24 Cr CHROMIUM 51.9961	25 Mn MANGANESE 54.938	26 Fe IRON 55.845	27 Co COBALT 58.933	28 Ni NICKEL 58.6934	29 Cu COPPER 63.546	30 Zn ZINC 65.38	31 Ga GALLIUM 69.723	32 Ge GERMANIUM 72.63	33 As ARSENIC 74.921	34 Se SELENIUM 78.971	35 Br BROMINE 79.904	36 Kr KRYPTON 83.7
37 Rb RUBIDIUM 85.467	38 Sr STRONTIUM 87.62	39 Y YTTRIUM 88.9058	40 Zr ZIRCONIUM 91.224	41 Nb NIOBIUM 92.9063	42 Mo MOLYBDENUM 95.95	43 Tc TECHNETIUM (98)	44 Ru RUTHENIUM 101.07	45 Rh RHODIUM 102.90	46 Pd PALLADIUM 106.42	47 Ag SILVER 107.8682	48 Cd CADMIUM 112.414	49 In INDIUM 114.818	50 Sn TIN 118.710	51 Sb ANTIMONY 121.760	52 Te TELLURIUM 127.60	53 I IODINE 126.90	54 Xe XENON 131.1
55 Cs CAESIUM 132.905	56 Ba BARIUM 137.327	57-71 *	72 Hf HAFNIUM 178.49	73 Ta TANTALUM 180.94	74 W TUNGSTEN 183.84	75 Re RHENIUM 186.207	76 Os OSMIUM 190.23	77 Ir IRIDIUM 192.217	78 Pt PLATINUM 195.084	79 Au GOLD 196.96	80 Hg MERCURY 200.59	81 Tl THALLIUM 204.38	82 Pb LEAD 207.2	83 Bi BISMUTH 208.98	84 Po POLONIUM (209)	85 At ASTATINE (210)	86 Rn RADON (22)
87 Fr FRANCIUM (223)	88 Ra RADIUM (226)	89-103 **	104 Rf RUTHERFORDIUM (267)	105 Db DUBNIUM (268)	106 Sg SEABORGIUM (271)	107 Bh BOHRIUM (272)	108 Hs HASSIUM (270)	109 Mt MEITNERIUM (276)	110 Ds DARMSTADTIUM (281)	111 Rg ROENTGENIUM (280)	112 Cn COPERNICIUM (285)	113 Uut UNUNTRIUM (284)	114 Fl FLEROVIUM (289)	115 Uup UNUNPENTIUM (288)	116 Lv LIVERMORIUM (293)	117 Uus UNUNSEPTIUM (294)	118 Uuo UNUNOCTIUM (29)

*	57 La LANTHANUM 138.90	58 Ce CERIUM 140.116	59 Pr PRASEODYMIUM 140.90	60 Nd NEODYMIUM 144.242	61 Pm PROMETHIUM (145)	62 Sm SAMARIUM 150.36	63 Eu EUROPIUM 151.964	64 Gd GADOLINIUM 157.25	65 Tb TERIBIUM 158.92	66 Dy DYSPROSIUM 162.500	67 Ho HOLMIUM 164.93	68 Er ERBIUM 167.259	69 Tm THULIUM 168.93	70 Yb YTTERBIUM 173.054	71 Lu LUTETIUM 174.9668
**	89 Ac ACTINIUM (227)	90 Th THORIUM 232.0377	91 Pa PROTACTINIUM 231.03	92 U URANIUM 238.02	93 Np NEPTUNIUM (237)	94 Pu PLUTONIUM (244)	95 Am AMERICIUM (243)	96 Cm CURIUM (247)	97 Bk BERKELIUM (247)	98 Cf CALIFORNIUM (251)	99 Es EINSTEINIUM (252)	100 Fm FERMIUM (257)	101 Md MENDELEVIUM (258)	102 No NOBELIUM (259)	103 Lr LAWRENCIUM (262)

The table is divided into groups in order to assist chemists working with these elements to learn and product how an element may behave or react in certain situations.

This table lists the name and abbreviation for each element. You may find some abbreviations easy to remember, such as H which is the abbreviation for hydrogen but some like iron (Fe) and gold (Au) are a somewhat more difficult to remember. In the instance of gold, "Au" originates from "aurum", which is the Latin word for gold.

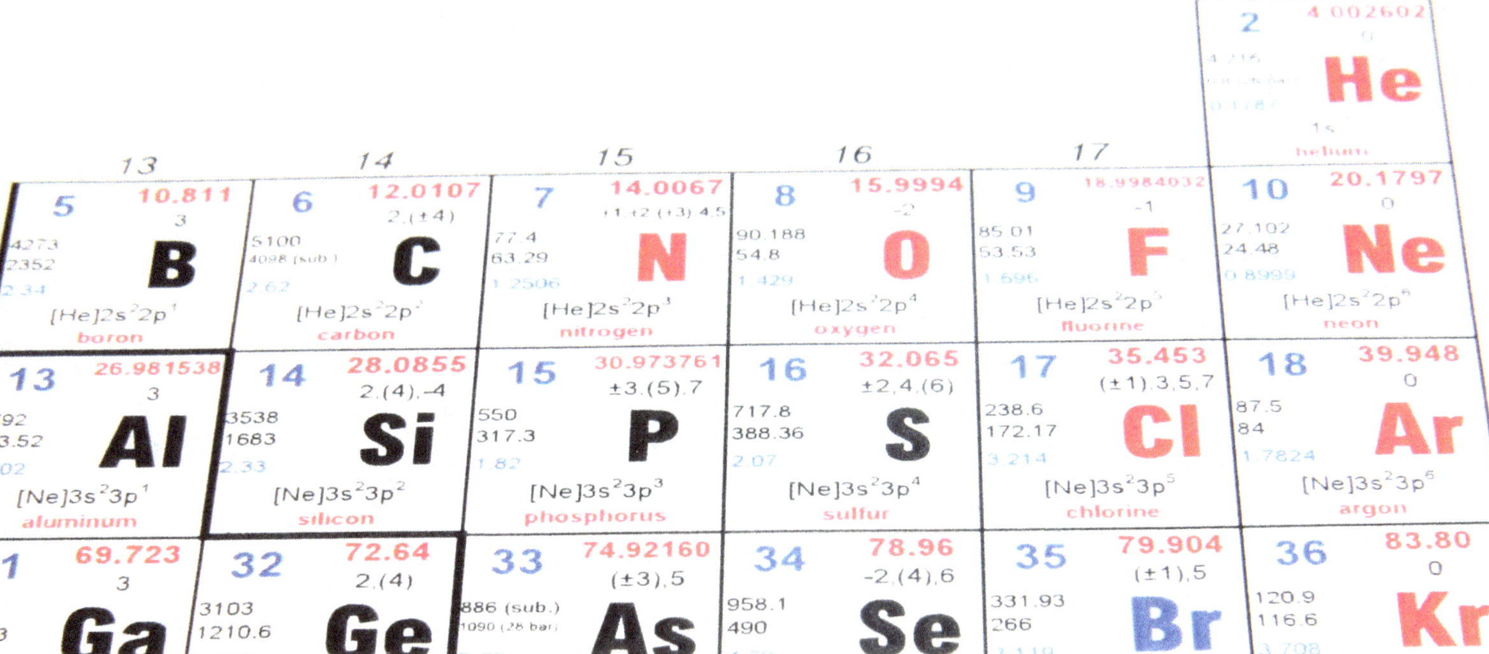

18
2   4.002602
He
helium
1s

13   14   15   16   17
5   10.811   6   12.0107   7   14.0067   8   15.9994   9   18.9984032   10   20.1797
B   C   N   O   F   Ne
[He]2s²2p¹   [He]2s²2p²   [He]2s²2p³   [He]2s²2p⁴   [He]2s²2p⁵   [He]2s²2p⁶
boron   carbon   nitrogen   oxygen   fluorine   neon

13   26.981538   14   28.0855   15   30.973761   16   32.065   17   35.453   18   39.948
Al   Si   P   S   Cl   Ar
[Ne]3s²3p¹   [Ne]3s²3p²   [Ne]3s²3p³   [Ne]3s²3p⁴   [Ne]3s²3p⁵   [Ne]3s²3p⁶
aluminum   silicon   phosphorus   sulfur   chlorine   argon

31   69.723   32   72.64   33   74.92160   34   78.96   35   79.904   36   83.80
Ga   Ge   As   Se   Br   Kr
[Ar]4s²3d¹⁰4p¹   [Ar]4s²3d¹⁰4p²   [Ar]4s²3d¹⁰4p³   [Ar]4s²3d¹⁰4p⁴   [Ar]4s²3d¹⁰4p⁵   [Ar]4s²3d¹⁰4p⁶
gallium   germanium   arsenic   selenium   bromine   krypton

49   114.818   50   118.71   51   121.76   52   127.60   53   126.90447   54   131.293
In   Sn   Sb   Te   I   Xe
[Kr]5s²4d¹⁰5p¹   [Kr]5s²4d¹⁰5p²   [Kr]5s²4d¹⁰5p³   [Kr]5s²4d¹⁰5p⁴   [Kr]5s²4d¹⁰5p⁵   [Kr]5s²4d¹⁰5p⁶
indium   tin   antimony   tellurium   iodine   xenon

81   204.3833   82   207.2   83   208.98038   84   [208.9824]   85   [209.9871]   86   [222.01]

NITROGEN
N
7
14.007

You can learn more by researching on the internet or by reaching out to your teachers, parents, and friends for additional information.

Visit

BABY PROFESSOR
EDUCATION KIDS

www.BabyProfessorBooks.com

to download Free Baby Professor eBooks
and view our catalog of new and exciting
Children's Books

www.ingramcontent.com/pod-product-compliance
Lightning Source LLC
Chambersburg PA
CBHW060223120726
48009CB00003B/118